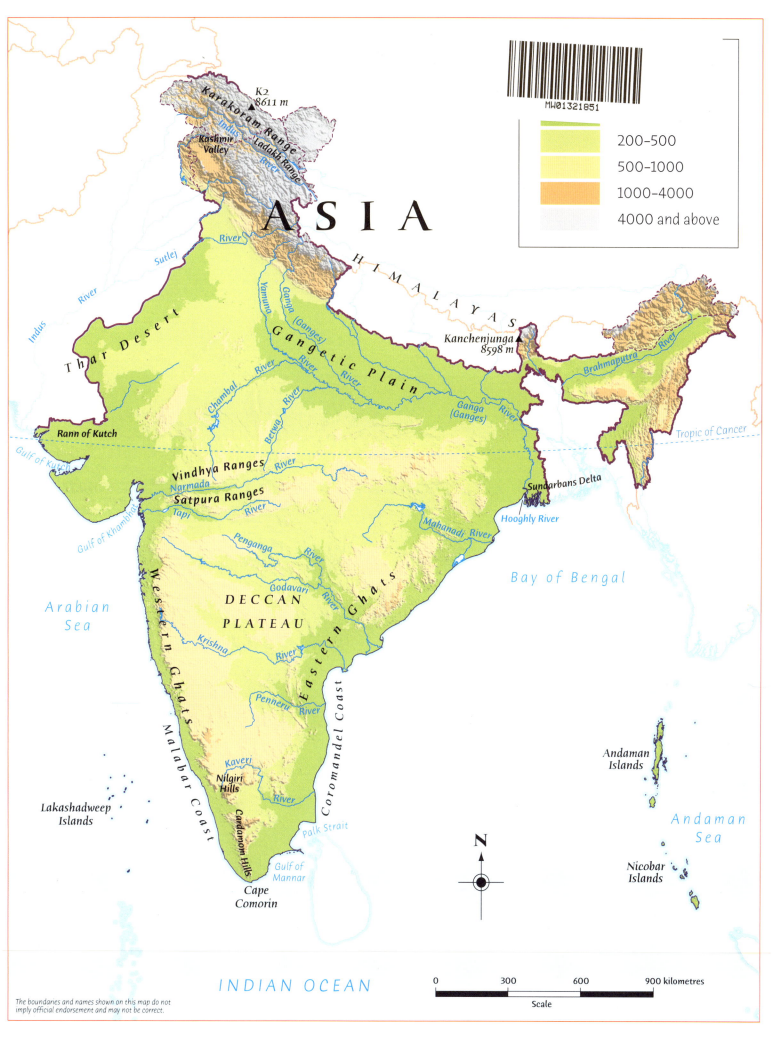

INDIA
Land, Life and Culture

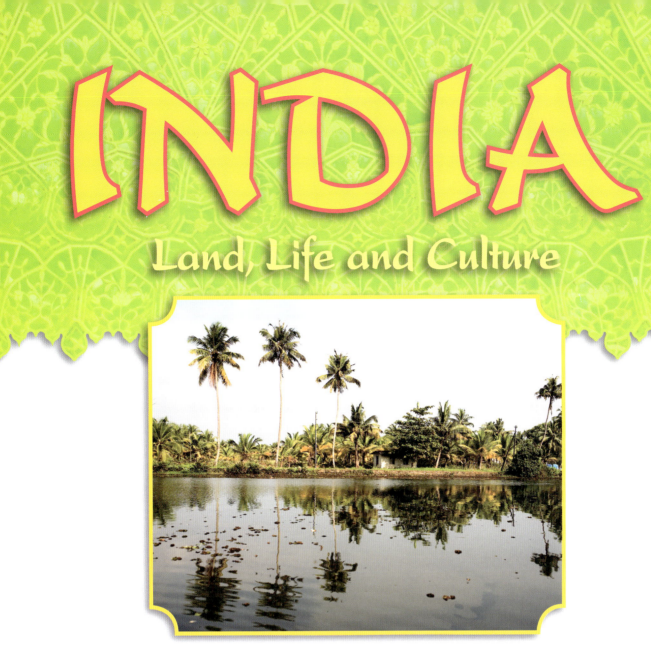

Land and Climate

ROSEMARY SACHDEV

MACMILLAN
LIBRARY

First published in 2009 by
MACMILLAN EDUCATION AUSTRALIA PTY LTD
15–19 Claremont Street, South Yarra 3141

Visit our website at www.macmillan.com.au or go directly to www.macmillanlibrary.com.au

Associated companies and representatives throughout the world.

Copyright © Rosemary Sachdev 2009

All rights reserved.
Except under the conditions described in the *Copyright Act 1968* of Australia and subsequent amendments, no part of this publication may be reproduced, stored in a retrieval system, or transmitted in any form or by any means, electronic, mechanical, photocopying, recording or otherwise, without the prior written permission of the copyright owner.

Educational institutions copying any part of this book for educational purposes under the Act must be covered by a Copyright Agency Limited (CAL) licence for educational institutions and must have given a remuneration notice to CAL. Licence restrictions must be adhered to. Any copies must be photocopies only, and they must not be hired out or sold. For details of the CAL licence contact: Copyright Agency Limited, Level 15, 233 Castlereagh Street, Sydney, NSW 2000. Telephone: (02) 9394 7600. Facsimile: (02) 9394 7601. Email: info@copyright.com.au

National Library of Australia Cataloguing-in-Publication data

Sachdev, Rosemary.
   Land and climate / Rosemary Sachdev.

   ISBN 978 1 4202 6715 0
   Sachdev, Rosemary. India: Land, life and culture.
   Includes index.
   Target Audience: For primary school age.
   Land use – India – Juvenile literature. India – Climate – Juvenile literature.

954

Edited by Kath Kovac
Text and cover design by Peter Shaw
Page layout by Kerri Wilson
Photo research by Lesya Bryndzia
Illustrations by Damien Demaj, DEMAP

Printed in China

Acknowledgements
Dedicated to Jasbir, who gave me India, and to Arkin, Amaya and Naira who belong and who will read these books some day.

With special thanks to the Archaeological Survey of India in New Delhi and Aurangabad for permission to take photographs in the Ajanta Caves with a camera and tripod, and thanks to the National Museum of India, Janpath, New Delhi for permission to photograph replicas in the Museum shop. Lastly, many thanks to La Boutique, Sunder Nagar, New Delhi, for the photograph of their joint family and their help in allowing us to photograph prints, paintings and artefacts from their collection.

With many thanks to all those who gave time for photographs and interviews, for lending their children to be photographed and for helping in the many ways they did and especial thanks to Jatinder, without whose tireless travel and wonderful photographs, these books would never have happened.

All photographs courtesy of Jatinder Marwaha except for:
AAP/AP Photo/Siddharth Darshan Kumar, **25**; Alamy/Edward North, **11** (bottom); Deepesh Kumar/Dreamstime, **9**; Sebastian D'Souza/AFP/Getty Images, **24**; Manan Vatsyayana/AFP/Getty Images, **11** (top); Michael Chen/iStockphoto, **28**; Beejal Mehta/iStockphoto, **18**; Ron Sumners/iStockphoto, **5**; Collection of RJ Sachdev, **12** (bottom), **26** (middle), **27** (middle top); Wikipedia/Nasa/Jesse Allen, **3**, **15**.

While every care has been taken to trace and acknowledge copyright, the publisher tenders their apologies for any accidental infringement where copyright has proved untraceable. Where the attempt has been unsuccessful, the publisher welcomes information that would redress the situation.

Contents

India, a land of diversity	4
The land	5
The beginning of India	6
Seas and coasts	8
Rivers	10
Plains	12
Plateaus and deltas	14
Mountains and hills	16
Deserts	20
Forests	22
Climate	24
Natural disasters	28
Environmental problems and solutions	30
Glossary	31
Index	32

Showing respect
Indian people always use titles with people's names to be polite, such as Shri and Shrimati if speaking Hindi, the national language, or Mr and Mrs if speaking English. These titles are different all over India, and their form depends on the family relationship or the seniority of the person addressed.

Glossary Words
When a word is printed in **bold**, you can look up its meaning in the Glossary on page 31.

India, a land of diversity

India is a land of great **diversity**, which can be seen in its arts, culture, people, landscape and climates. For every description of Indian life, there are many different but equally true variations.

India has a very long history. People have lived in India for around 10 000 years and come from many different racial backgrounds. They speak hundreds of languages; some spoken by millions of Indians, others spoken by only a few thousand. The country has many different landscapes and climates, from freezing mountains to hot, tropical areas.

India came under British influence in the 1600s, and Britain took control of India in the 1850s. India gained its independence from Britain in 1947 and became a **republic** in 1950.

Ancient carvings

Mountainous landscapes

Majestic tombs

Many religions

Unique plants

Wild animals

This book explains the different areas of India and how climate affects the land. It also looks at how the land and climate have affected the people who live there.

The land

India is a land of many climates. It can be hot and dry, hot and wet, cold and dry or cold and wet. Many different land formations and forests are also found in India. It has very high, cold mountains and warmer hills. It has tropical rainforests, plains surrounding large rivers, rocky **plateaus**, dry thorny forests and deserts.

Mountains and hills

India has the highest mountain range in the world, and hills that are 2000 to 3000 metres high. The climate is mild in the hills, but very cold in the mountains, which may have snow all year.

Deserts

India has hot, dry deserts and cold, dry deserts in areas that receive very little rainfall. The cold deserts are in the high mountains.

Plateau

The centre of India is described as a plateau. It is rocky, almost flat and has a harsh hot climate all year.

For Your Information

The people of India have had to adapt to every type of climate. In the villages, where most Indians live, people often have to do without electricity. They have to find natural ways of keeping cool or warm.

India's landscapes range from cold mountains to hot deserts and tropical forests.

The beginning of India

More than 100 million years ago, India and Australia were joined to a vast landmass called Gondwana, named after an area in central India.

Separation of India from Gondwana

When Gondwana broke apart, Australia floated east to where it is now. India travelled faster to the north and banged against China about 70 million years ago. The impact was so strong that the land between them rose and formed the great mountain range of the Himalayas, which includes Mount Everest. Sea shells and marine fossils are still found in the lower mountains of the Himalayas.

Gondwana started to break up about 200 million years ago, forming many continents, including South Asia, Australia and the Indonesian islands.

For Your Information

The Earth's continental plates are still moving slightly in the region where India joined the Asian continent. This causes frequent earthquakes in the mountain regions.

India today

India now looks like an upside down triangle hanging from the great Asian land mass, with projections on both sides. The pointed end of the Indian triangle projects into three seas: the Arabian Sea to the west, the Indian Ocean to the south, and the Bay of Bengal to the east.

India moved to its present position about 70 million years ago.

Bordering countries

India shares borders with eight countries. Pakistan is to the west, Burma (Myanmar) is to the east, and China, Tibet and Bhutan are to the north. Afghanistan just touches India to the north and Bangladesh has a long border with India in the east.

Except for China and Tibet, all these countries, with the island countries of Sri Lanka and the Maldives, form the South Asian Association for Regional Cooperation (SAARC). SAARC was formed in 1985 and its main purpose is cooperation in economic and political matters. Afghanistan became a member in 2007.

For Your Information

Bangladesh is surrounded by India on three sides and by the Bay of Bengal to the south. India has seven states to the east of Bangladesh that have boundaries with Burma (Myanmar).

India shares borders with eight other countries.

Seas and coasts

India is surrounded by three seas and has a very long coastline containing sandy beaches, mangrove swamps, rocky outcrops and **delta** regions. The land is very low along the coast. It never rises more than 150 metres above sea level.

Beaches

All the beaches in India have fishing villages and are famous for their fishermen. Many of the beaches now have hotels that are popular with European tourists. They like to come to India in winter, as the coastal areas are always hot and good for swimming.

The Ghats

Inland from India's west coast is a long line of low hills called the Western Ghats. The Eastern Ghats run in a broken line of hills down the east coast. A number of the Indian rivers flow through the Eastern Ghats to the sea.

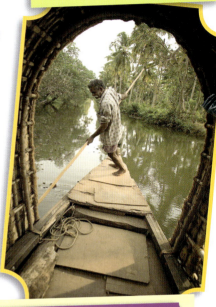

Tourists enjoy taking boat rides on Kerala's lagoons.

For Your Information

Between the Western Ghats and the sea are many lagoons. The state of Kerala relies greatly on tourists taking boat rides on the lagoons, which helps Kerala's economy.

Tourist hotels cannot be built within 100 metres of any beach, such as this one in Goa, to preserve land near the beach from harmful development.

Island groups

India has two groups of islands some way from its coast. The Andaman and Nicobar group is to the east, and the Lakshadweep Island group is to the west.

The Andaman and Nicobar group

This group contains about 300 volcanic islands, which are hilly with thick forests. Only a few islands have people living on them, and these people still live a simple life. They grow fruits and some cash crops, and have some small industries.

The island furthest to the north is quite close to Burma (Myanmar), and the southernmost island almost touches Indonesia.

For Your Information

The capital of the Andaman and Nicobar island group, Port Blair, once had a large jail that held political prisoners when the British ruled India. Most of the people living on these islands are descended from those prisoners. The original people of the islands still live in tribal villages.

The Lakshadweep Islands

The Lakshadweep Island group consists of about 35 coral islands, but only 10 have people living on them. The people grow coconut palms and make coir, catch fish or grow fruit. Tourism is now popular on these islands.

Port Blair's prison was called the cellular gaol because of its shape.

Rivers

The water in India's longest northern rivers comes from melting snow in the Himalayan mountains. The rivers flow from the mountains down to the Bay of Bengal.

India's southern rivers also flow into the Bay of Bengal after cutting through the Eastern Ghats. Some of India's other important rivers flow into the Arabian Sea.

The Ganga

The Ganga is India's most famous river. It is considered holy by Hindus, who believe the water purifies whatever flows into it. Many Hindu religious sites are on the banks of the Ganga river.

The river starts in the mountains at Gangotri, which is a place of **pilgrimage**. The last part of the Ganga flows through Bangladesh before it reaches the Bay of Bengal. A branch of the Ganga, called the Hooghly, flows through the Sunderbans, a large delta area in West Bengal and Bangladesh.

Varanasi, on the banks of the Ganga River, is Hinduism's most sacred town.

The Yamuna

The Yamuna River also starts in the Himalayas. It joins the Ganga at a town called Allahabad, in India's north. The place where the two rivers meet in Allahabad is another sacred place for Hindus.

The Brahmaputra

The Brahmaputra is the longest river in India. It starts in Tibet and flows east, south and west before it reaches Assam in India's north-east. It joins the Ganga in Bangladesh and flows down to the Bay of Bengal.

Central and southern rivers

The central rivers flow into the Arabian Sea. The southern rivers flow into the Bay of Bengal to the east. Most start in the Western Ghats, flow right across India and cut through the Eastern Ghats to the sea. All these rivers rely on the **monsoon** for their water.

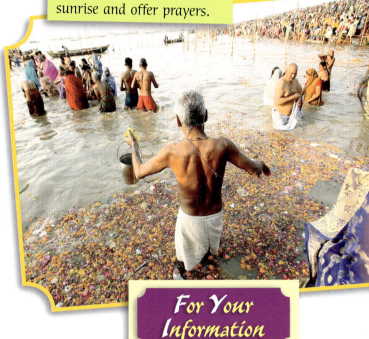

At the Kumbh Mela, people bathe in the river at sunrise and offer prayers.

For Your Information

Great fairs called melas are held every year where the Ganga meets the Yamuna. The Kumbh Mela is held there every 12 years, and Hindus try to attend this fair at least once.

The Brahmaputra, India's longest river, is 2900 kilometres long.

Plains

India's river plains are very **fertile.** When the flood water recedes after the monsoon, very rich soil is left behind. Food and cash crops such as sugar cane are grown in this soil, which can support two or more crops a year. Many canals run from the rivers to the plains, supplying water for irrigation.

Rice and wheat are grown at different times of the year in the northern plain.

The food bowl of India

One of India's northern rivers, the Sutlej, flows through Punjab and has many canals running through the plains. This is the richest land in the country, and is known as the food bowl of India. All the main food crops, such as wheat, rice, sugar, fruit and vegetables are grown here.

The Gangetic Plain

The Gangetic Plain, which surrounds the Ganga river, is very densely populated. Two of India's largest states, Uttar Pradesh and Bihar, are on the plain. Many hundreds of millions of people live here. The climate is extreme, ranging from very hot in summer to cold in winter and very wet in the monsoon months.

For Your Information

Half of the rich and fertile state of Punjab is now in Pakistan, through which four major rivers and many canals run. Indian Punjab still grows much of India's food crops since new canals were built.

Most of the Gangetic Plain's population lives in villages of only a few thousand people.

Industries in the plains

The plains are important to India because they are fairly flat, making transport easy. Great lengths of roads and railways carry goods. Many industries, such as iron, steel, cement and paper manufacturing have been set up in the plains.

Textiles

Textiles are a major source of income in India. Wool mills are found in the Punjab plains. Many cotton and silk weaving factories provide employment throughout India.

Other industries

Other plains industries include sportsgoods, leatherwork, electronics, sugar factories and car and aeroplane manufacture.

Did You Know?

India is the largest producer of sugar cane in the world.

For Your Information

Despite the variety of industries found in the plains, most people living there rely on domestic animals, such as cows and goats, and growing a few crops on their small amount of land, for their survival.

Silk sari weavers take about two weeks to make one sari.

MEET E. Manickam

E. Manickam is a silk weaver who lives in Little Kancheepuram. He has been weaving since he was two years old.

In conversation with E. Manickam

I learned the craft of weaving from my father, and I have taught my wife and two of my daughters. I like creating beauty; it gives me joy when people admire my work. But I don't think my grandchildren will do this work. It's very hard and doesn't pay well. I hope my grandchildren will get good jobs.

Plateaus and deltas

Plateaus are fairly flat areas that are higher than the surrounding land. In India, they are usually dry and rocky. Deltas are flat areas of land where rivers break up into smaller streams before entering the sea.

The Deccan Plateau

The Deccan Plateau runs from the centre of India to the south. The plateau is separated from the sea by the Western Ghats and Eastern Ghats.

Mining

In rocky areas of the plateau, coal, iron, copper and limestone are mined. The Kolar gold mine in the Deccan Plateau once produced all of India's gold. Gold was first mined there in 100 CE, with major production starting in 1850. The mine closed in 2003.

Crops and vegetation

The soil of the Deccan Plateau is either black or red, and is fertile. Cotton, sugar cane and peanuts are grown in this region. Some areas have thick forests. The wood from these trees is used for building and furniture.

Did You Know?

Indians are very fond of gold ornaments. Gold now has to be imported to meet the demand, as the old system of mining has depleted India's natural gold reserves.

Plateau rocks often look as though they might tumble down at any time.

This Deccan landscape near Aurangabad shows the black soil in which crops can grow after the monsoon.

The Sunderbans Delta

The Sunderbans Delta region is found where the Ganga and the Brahmaputra rivers meet, slow down and deposit **silt** before reaching the sea. The rivers break up into small streams, forming islands and mud flats in the delta region before reaching the sea. The water is both fresh and salty.

In the monsoon season, the whole delta area is often under water, and ships can sail through the delta to Kolkata, the capital of West Bengal.

The few people living in the Sunderbans rely on fishing and gathering honey or wood from the trees for their income.

The Royal Bengal tiger

The Sunderbans Delta is home to the Royal Bengal tiger, which has some different characteristics to other Indian tigers. It swims as often as it walks on land. The mud makes hunting more difficult for the tiger, and the scent of other animals is washed away by the tides.

For Your Information

Few people live in the Sunderbans Delta, so the Royal Bengal tiger has never feared humans. For safety reasons, the men often wear a face mask on the back of their heads to confuse the tigers.

The Sunderbans Delta is on the world heritage list because it is the largest delta and has the largest mangrove swamp in the world.

Mountains and hills

India has many mountains and hills, ranging in height from less than 2000 metres to more than 6000 metres in the Himalayan Mountains, the highest mountain range in the world.

The Greater Himalayas

The Greater Himalayas, in the north of India, have an average height of more than 6000 metres. The highest Indian peak, Kanchanjanga, is 8598 metres high. The Greater Himalayas are covered with snow all year, so nothing grows there.

Did You Know?
The word Himalaya comes from the Sanskrit language, and means 'the abode of snow'.

The Middle Himalayas

The Middle Himalayas are about 2000 metres high and have beautiful valleys where pine, fir, oak and deodar trees grow. The British set up many 'hill stations' in the Middle Himalayas when they ruled India. These hill stations, such as Shimla, Naini Tal and Darjeeling, served as cool retreats in summer, away from the terrible heat of the plains.

The Outer Himalayas

Much of the Outer Himalayas is covered with thick forests of chesnut, laurel, pine and bamboo. Many wildlife sanctuaries are found here. Some forest has now been cleared for cash crops such as sugar cane.

This snowy pine forest is in Kashmir, in the Middle Himalayas.

Ladakh is a cold desert region with mountains covered with snow.

Kashmir

Kashmir has a beautiful valley containing lakes surrounded by the mountains of the Middle Himalayas. Kashmiri people are famous for their shawls, embroidery, **papier mâché** and articles made from walnut wood.

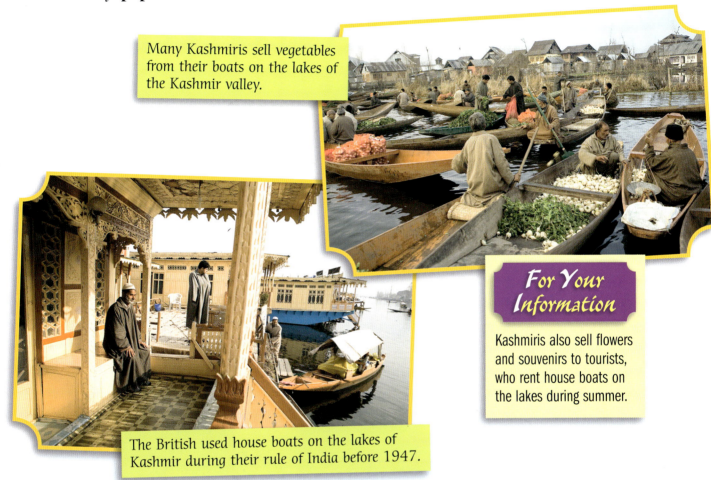

Many Kashmiris sell vegetables from their boats on the lakes of the Kashmir valley.

For Your Information

Kashmiris also sell flowers and souvenirs to tourists, who rent house boats on the lakes during summer.

The British used house boats on the lakes of Kashmir during their rule of India before 1947.

MEET Haji Khazar Mohammed Pala

Haji Khazar Mohammed Pala is a houseboat owner who has been working in the family-run hospitality business since early childhood.

In conversation with Haji Khazar Mohammed Pala

I enjoy my work, as I meet people from around the world. Ours is an ancestral business and I hope my children will also work in the same line. We are busy with tourists from March till October. My name, Haji, means I have been on the pilgrimage to **Mecca**. I could only go on this pilgrimage when my family was provided for and I was free from debt.

Smaller mountains and hills

There are many other hills in India that do not reach the height of the Himalayas. The Satpura Ranges and the Vindhya Ranges cut across India from west to east, but these hills are mostly below 2000 metres.

The southern hills

The Cardamom Hills are at the meeting point of the Western Ghats and the Eastern Ghats. The Nilgiri (blue) Hills are in the south of India. Hill stations in the Nilgiri Hills include Ootacamund, called Ooty for short, and Kodaikanal. The good climate at these hill stations makes them popular holiday destinations.

Plantations

Rubber, tea, coffee and spices such as pepper are grown in the southern hills. Cinchona trees, the bark of which is used for making quinine, a medicine for people with malaria, are also grown here.

Small holiday cottages line the slopes at the Ooty hill station.

The eastern Himalayas and the north-eastern hills

Darjeeling is the main town in the eastern Himalayas. The north-eastern hills are an important group of hills in India. They do not get snow, but rainfall is very heavy there.

The Darjeeling variety of tea is grown in plantations around Darjeeling, an important hill station in the east of India.

Tribal people of the north-eastern hills

Seven north-eastern states are separated from the rest of India by Bangladesh, and were originally inhabited only by tribal people. Each of the main tribal groups has its own state. Two of the main tribal groups are the Khasis and the Nagas.

Most of the tribal people living there became Christians more than 100 years ago. Before that, they were nature worshippers. Some still keep to their old religion. They all still wear their tribal clothing for special occasions such as Christmas or weddings.

For Your Information

Khasi children take the name of their mother, not their father. India does not have social security programs, so the family take responsibility for older members.

MEET June Pariat

June Pariat belongs to the Khasi tribe. She is the eldest of three sisters and three brothers in Shillong, the capital of Meghalaya. She worked as a radio announcer for western music on All India Radio, then as a newsreader and editor for Khasi and Garo news in Meghalaya.

In conversation with June Pariat

Khasi society is matrilineal. Property passes from mother to youngest daughter, who is the custodian of the family property and has the duty of caring for older or less privileged members of the family. The head of the family is still the man, but women are respected. In Khasi society, tradition goes hand in hand with modernity.

Deserts

India has two very different sorts of deserts; the hot, dry deserts of Rajasthan in the west, and the cold, dry desert of Ladakh in the northern mountains.

The Thar Desert

The Thar Desert in Rajasthan has a typical hot desert climate. It is very hot during the day and cold at night.

Thar Desert people

Thar desert people have colourful clothes. The men wear large red or orange turbans. The women wear long skirts, usually red, and embroidered blouses that often have mirrors and shells attached. The women sew very elaborate embroidery for wall-hangings and household use.

Did You Know? Much of Rajasthan is covered by sand dunes that change shape with the strong desert winds.

Rann of Kutch

South of the desert of Rajasthan is the Rann of Kutch. The land here is very arid and salty. Nothing can grow in the baked clay and mud flats. The Rann has a population of very hardy people, who survive by mining salt. They are partly **nomadic** and also herd camels and sheep.

Camels are often used as transport in the deserts of Rajasthan.

Jaisalmer Fort is one of Rajasthan's wonderful forts and palaces, which are designed to keep out the harsh weather.

Ladakh

Ladakh is a cold desert region to the north of the Kashmir valley. Several trade routes used to run through Ladakh to China, but these are now closed. China has now occupied about one-third of Ladakh.

Buddhist monasteries seem to grow out of the rocky land in Ladakh.

Ladakh people

The people of Ladakh are Buddhists. Most of the Ladakhis are nomadic herders. Tourism and trekking have recently become popular. Although only a few people are involved, much of Ladakh's income now comes from tourism.

Climate and agriculture

There is almost no rainfall in Ladakh. The average is less than 250 millimetres a year. Channels have been built to carry water for crops from the melting ice and snow in the mountains. At heights of 3000 to 4000 metres, only barley and wheat can grow, and only for about three months per year. Some fruit is grown in the lower areas.

Wildlife

There is some bird life in Ladakh, as they pass through and rest when migrating to and from Siberia. The only native animals are the snow leopard, yak, lynx, ibex and the Tibetan antelope, which is highly endangered.

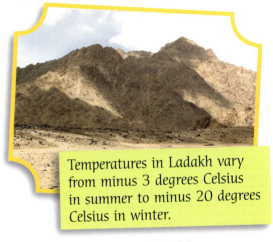

Temperatures in Ladakh vary from minus 3 degrees Celsius in summer to minus 20 degrees Celsius in winter.

Yaks are used to transport goods and people, and they also provide milk that is used for drinking and making cheese.

Forests

India has every kind of forest cover, from alpine to tropical rainforest and every variety in between. About one-fifth of the land is covered in forest.

Deciduous forests

Deciduous trees are found across India. Some of these trees shed their leaves at the end of winter and still have new leaves by spring. Teak and sheesham wood are used for building and furniture. Peepul trees have religious associations for Hindus and Buddhists.

Peepul trees often have a shrine to Hindu gods at their base.

Tropical thorny forests

Tropical thorny trees grow in the centre of India. They have few leaves, rough thick bark and long roots. They need less water to survive than other trees. Kikar and babul trees are the most common.

Tropical thorny forests may have many trees but offer little shade.

For Your Information

Depending on the **altitude** and the rainfall, different types of trees grow in different regions of India. The wood and leaves of some trees are used for fuel, as well as feeding animals such as goats.

Mangrove swamps

India's long coast line has many mangrove swamps scattered along it. They help protect the land from storms and erosion as well as from **tsunamis**.

Mangroves grow in salty water and have long, thin trunks that are covered by water when the tide comes in.

Tropical rainforests

Tropical rainforests grow along the Western Ghats and in the north-eastern hills. These trees never lose their leaves, so they are known as evergreen. Trees such as ebony and rosewood also grow in the southern states.

Rainforests grow in the north-eastern hills, an area where the rainfall is very heavy.

Alpine forests

Alpine forests grow in the higher areas of the north east, depending on the altitude. They only grow between 2500 and 4000 metres. Alpine forests are found in the Himalayan regions of the north, where the temperatures are very low. The trees are mostly pines and firs and are never bare of their thin, needle-like leaves.

The wood of pine trees is used for building and furniture.

Climate

India has four main climatic regions. However, many variations in climate occur, depending on the height above sea level, the rainfall and the distance from the sea.

The Himalayan mountain range has a major effect on India's climate. It stops the cold Arctic winds sweeping down from China. It also traps the rains of the monsoon, which are India's main source of rainfall.

Rainfall and the monsoon

The main monsoon comes from the south west and hits India's south-west coast in early June. The monsoon rain takes about a month to spread from the south-west coast, where it first strikes India, up to the north-west, by which time it has covered the whole country.

The monsoon lasts three to four months and then gradually leaves India, taking about a month to recede. The north is usually dry by September, but the south and south-west still get rain till October.

The dry season

Once the main monsoon is over, almost no rain falls for the rest of the year, except for a second monsoon that reaches the north-east of India in November. Dust storms are common in the hot, dry summer of the northern plains, before the monsoon starts, and in desert regions. In the north, irrigation has made the land greener, so that dust storms are now less common. Instead, thunderstorms come, but very little rain falls.

Did You Know? Cherrapunji, a plateau area of Meghalaya, is the wettest place in the world. It has an annual rainfall of more than 11 metres.

Dust storm such as this one are less common than they used to be.

Temperature

In the northern winter, temperatures vary from minus 10 degrees Celsius at night to about 25 degrees Celsius during the day in January. In April, most of India has temperatures of about 30 degrees Celsius, except for the hill areas, which have temperatures of about 20 degrees Celsius. By May, the plains have temperatures well over 40 degrees Celsius every day.

For Your Information

Once the monsoon has covered India, temperatures are usually about 32 degrees Celsius, but can reach more than 40 degrees Celsius if there has been less rain than normal. From October, when the monsoon has gone, the temperatures drop to between 25 and 30 degrees Celsius.

Humidity

During and just after the monsoon, the humidity is very high and can reach 100 per cent. This is very uncomfortable. Many Indians in the north prefer high temperatures and low humidity.

In the coastal regions and areas in the south, where temperatures remain fairly constant in the 30s, the humidity is always high. In areas where temperatures rise higher, the humidity is lower, except during the monsoon season.

Monsoon rainstorms can flood streets, causing damage to cars and homes.

Designing houses for the climate

Indian houses have always been designed with the extremes of India's climate in mind. The standard design of traditional houses keeps them as cool as possible in summer or as warm as possible in winter, depending on their location.

Traditional city houses in India have rooms extending from an inner courtyard. The outside walls facing the street are always bare, except for the entrance door. Most traditional village houses have only one or two rooms. Many houses have no electricity, so much of the people's life is lived outside.

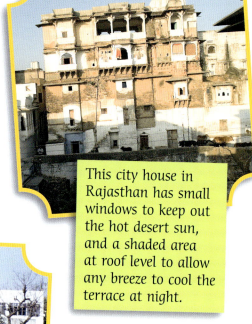

This city house in Rajasthan has small windows to keep out the hot desert sun, and a shaded area at roof level to allow any breeze to cool the terrace at night.

A north Indian bungalow usually has a flat roof, and its central rooms have high windows so that rising hot air can escape.

Bungalows

When the British ruled India, they built bungalows with verandahs and gardens. The bungalow was developed from the Bengal house, or 'Bangla', which had a front verandah. This design is popular with Indians, who build bungalows wherever there is enough land.

Did You Know?

The design of the Australian bungalow house was developed by men of the British Army in India, who later took the design to Australia.

This old bungalow in Goa has a tiled sloping roof and verandahs all around the outside.

Traditional village houses

Each climatic region of India has its own style of traditional housing, which is designed to suit the climate.

Village houses

Houses in the hot, humid south are usually made of brick with sloping roofs to drain heavy rain. They also have large openings to allow fresh air inside.

Most of the east is hot and humid. The houses are made of brick with sloping tiled or thatch roofs and many will have verandahs.

North-eastern areas are warm to cold but always very wet. Timber or bamboo houses have sloping roofs and may be built on stilts. They have plenty of openings, and often have verandahs.

In the western desert, the days are very hot but the nights are cold. Thick brick or stone walls and thatch or stone slab roofs keep heat out of the house during the day and in at night. The houses have few or no windows.

In the northern hills it is cold, with rain and snow. Houses have thick stone walls with small openings. They often have two storeys with an outdoor stair. The animals are kept on the ground floor and the family live on top.

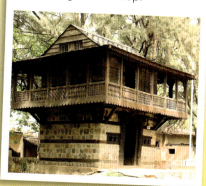

The northern plains are mostly hot and dry, except during the monsoon, when it is very wet. The houses have brick walls with flat roofs and small windows.

Natural disasters

India's people have coped with earthquakes, landslides, fires, floods, drought, cyclones and tsunamis for thousands of years. They have learned to manage life in spite of every disaster.

Earthquakes

India lies in a very active **seismic zone**, especially in the north. The Himalayan mountain range has frequent earthquakes that register more than 8 on the **Richter scale**. Earthquakes on the northern plains are not as strong. Kutch, in the west of India, also has frequent earthquakes that are sometimes very strong. Many buildings are damaged and lives lost due to earthquakes in India.

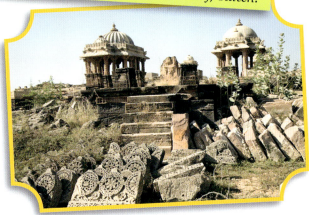

Pieces of buildings lie scattered around after a strong earthquake in Bhuj, Kutch.

Landslides

Landslides often occur in the hills. These may be due to earthquakes, very heavy monsoon rain or forest clearing. Roads are often blocked and houses may be buried in landslides.

For Your Information

Fires are common in the forests of India's north during the hot, dry summer months.

Floods

When the monsoon rains are heavy, large areas of India near its many rivers may experience floods. Village houses can be almost underwater. Food has to be sent to people sitting on their roof tops, surrounded by water. If the floods remain for some time, boats are sent to rescue people from these areas.

Monsoon rains have flooded this Indian village.

Drought and famine

The amount of rainfall in India is different every year. The monsoon is very unreliable, and sometimes fails completely. This can happen in any part of India. Each year, **meteorology** experts predict which areas are likely to receive less rain.

A change in wind patterns in the Arabian Sea can affect the monsoon. For example, an area preparing for heavy rain may experience drought. If there is a drought, no crops can grow. Parts of India suffered badly from **famine** in the past, but with rapid transport and government help, this no longer happens.

In this drought-hit area, the earth is so dry it has cracked and will not easily hold water even when it rains.

Cyclones

Cyclones occur along the coasts on the east and west, though more often in the east. Cyclone-affected areas are located all through the south as well. Houses, trees and crops are damaged by cyclone winds, which can reach 250 kilometres per hour.

Did You Know?

Since the 2004 tsunami, warning systems have been put into place. If another tsunami occurs, people will have more time to escape to higher ground.

The 2004 tsunami hit the south east coast of India, causing a great deal of damage.

Environmental problems and solutions

India is doing what it can to solve the many problems it faces as a result of global warming and the country's increasing population. These include loss of forests, less groundwater, shortage of energy and high fuel prices.

Reforestation

When trees are cut for a project such as road building, they are now replaced. However, it is difficult to protect young trees from the climate and animals, so at least ten trees are planted for each one cut.

For Your Information

In recent years, village women in the northern hills began hugging trees to defy the men who came to cut the trees down. This became famous as the 'chipko' (hugging) movement and has spread through large areas of the hills. The movement originally started in Rajasthan, a desert area with very few trees.

Rainwater harvesting and check dams

Indian people rely on groundwater from wells in areas where there are no rivers. Rainwater harvesting is now compulsory in many buildings. Water is collected from roofs during the monsoon and stored. People have also started building **check dams** to increase the water table and provide more water for the wells.

This micro-hydel power station in Ladakh generates small amounts of electricity from a natural watercourse to provide power for a village.

Wind energy can generate electricity or run pumps to move water; it is being used in many parts of India, especially in the deserts of Rajasthan.

Glossary

altitude	height above sea level
check dams	village ponds that have been enlarged and reinforced to allow water to be stored during the monsoon
delta	flat land, usually triangular in shape, through which a river takes many outlets to the sea
diversity	great variety
famine	a very bad shortage of food or water in a district
fertile	rich and productive
Mecca	the holy city that all Muslims want to visit at least once in a lifetime
meteorology	the science of weather
monsoon	a seasonal wind bringing heavy rain
nomadic	people without a fixed home, who drive animals from one place to another
papier mâché	paper pulp formed into shapes while wet and dried to a hard finish
pilgrimage	journey to a holy place or shrine
plateaus	large areas of fairly flat land that are higher than the surrounding areas
republic	form of government where the rulers are elected by the people and the leader is usually called the President
Richter scale	scale from 1 to 10, used for measuring earthquakes
seismic zone	an area which is prone to earthquakes
silt	deposit of mud or sand carried by flowing water and then deposited after flooding of a river recedes
tsunamis	series of waves caused by underwater earthquakes

Index

A
Andaman and Nicobar Islands 9
Arabian Sea 7, 11, 29

B
Bangladesh 7, 10, 19
Bay of Bengal 7, 10, 11
beaches 8
bordering countries 7
Brahmaputra River 11, 15
bungalows 26

C
China 6, 7, 21
climate 24, 25
cyclones 29

D
Deccan Plateau 14
delta 8, 14, 15
deserts 5, 20, 21
drought 29
dry season 24

E
earthquakes 28

F
famine 29
floods 24, 28
forests 5, 22, 23

G
Ganga River 10, 11, 12, 15
Gangetic Plain 12
Ghats 8, 10, 11, 18
global warming 30
Gondwana 6

H
hills 5, 16, 17, 18
Himalayas 6, 10, 11, 16, 18, 19, 28
houseboats 17
house design 26, 27
humidity 25
hydroelectricity 30

I
Indian Ocean 7
industries 13
islands 9

K
Kashmir 16, 17, 21

L
Ladakh 16, 20, 21
lagoons 8
Lakshadweep Islands 9
landslides 28

M
mangroves 23
mining 14
monsoon 11, 15, 24, 25, 28
Mount Everest 6
mountains 5, 6, 16, 17

N
nomadic people 20, 21

P
plains 12, 13
plateau 5, 14

R
rainfall 24
reforestation 30
rivers 10, 11
Royal Bengal tiger 15

S
Sunderbans Delta 10, 15

T
temperature 25
textiles 13
Thar Desert 20
tourism 8, 17, 21
trees 22, 23, 30
tribal people 19
tsunami 29

W
wells 30
wind energy 30

Y
yaks 21
Yamuna River 11